animals
of the ocean

Teresa O'Brien

D0746731

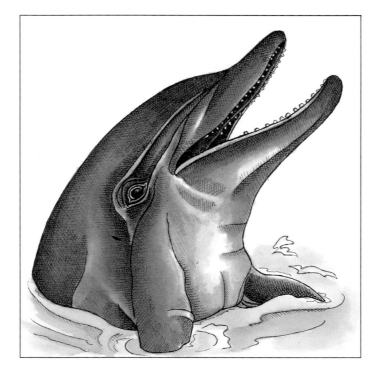

Flying Frog Publishing

Who am I,
the biggest animal in the
world?

Who am I?
I look like a fish,
but I am not a fish.

Who are we,
with thick fur coats
and flippers for feet?

Who are we,
birds that can fly under the
water but not in the sky?

Who am I,
with a shell on my back
and flippers for feet?

Which animals can
you spot?